Jobs for Finance Majors

G. Wainwright

About the Author

Gayron (Jaron) Wainwright lives full time in New Jersey. He has written a numerous amount of articles for The Motley Fool and the Yahoo! contributor network. The first acclaimed eBook he wrote was Izzy's Daydream, which he co-authored with his daughter Jayana Wainwright. He enjoys writing, learning, spending time with his daughters, going to church and lifting the name of Jesus, and making money.

Jobs for finance majors is a book for people who may want to explore different career opportunities. This is not a book just for students in High school or a freshmen in college, but it's for anyone who may want a change of career. A factory worker may want to go to college for the first time and may not know which major to take. I'm just trying to give them a chance to explore the fabulous world of finance and all that it offers. So you could be a factory worker who is tired of your job, bosses, or the strenuous work for such a little pay and you want to change your future outlook. A person working at Wendy's or McDonalds may want to get more for their knowledge because they know they are smart and should be making more money. Not everyone wants to work for minimum wage, so exploring different career paths before you decide is worth the time. This way you do not have to quit your job, you can just read about the opportunities on your free time.

Then you decide!

Table of Contents

About the Author

From the Author

Chapter 1: The World of Finance

Chapter 2: Required Education

Chapter 3: Job Opportunities

Chapter 4: Motley Fool Articles

Chapter 5: Salaries

Chapter 1: The World of Finance

We all know that the financial industry is a vitally dog-eat-dog profession, notably at the entry level. The office desks of financial professionals' are stockpiled high with the student's resumes. Students with enormous dreams of becoming the people with their hands on the scales, tipping it in the favor of their clients and employers. Along with those dreams of tipping the scales in their client and employer's favor, they also want the scales tipped in their favor as well. With the scales in their favor they can accumulate massive amounts of wealth and with wealth comes the cars, clothes, homes, and influential power over very important leaders. N Somewhere along the line they found out that hard work and determination could get them all of this by the age of 30.

Finance majors have a chance to enter the core inner workings of an organization. For finance majors there are a vast amount of divergent and awarding employment opportunities at their grasp. These divergent and awarding career opportunities range from handling money matters for small to big businesses that participate in selling financial products to managing financial departments. To go into more depth, you could aid a parent company or a subsidiary company in managing risks and price securities meticulously by employing finance, economic, and statistical skills. A finance major may also counsel clients on short-term and long-term investment methods, or they could be in a position to utilize a business's capital to buy and/or sell securities on capital markets. The finance majors can look forward to average salaries starting from $50,000 plus per annum.

These financial jobs are present at nearly every company in nearly every industry and sector. There are three ways to find opportunities—online, on-campus, and networking events—and it's a brilliant idea to utilize all three approaches. Take note that financial jobs are specially designed, so nonexclusive job boards wouldn't be the most desiring place to scout for such positions. Rather than looking on job boards, cogitate on niche sites. When searching around, specialized executive recruiters also known as headhunters will be priceless resources for both financial career advice and job opportunities. The alumni association at your university should also be very advantageous by connecting you with industry insiders who sometimes can give you some needed insight and quite often job leads.

Chapter 2: Required Education

We all know to get into the finance industry you have to have education or the experience. Sometimes you have to have both, the education and the experience combined. If you can get into a low level position and get promoted from within you may get in with just the experience. They used to say that you can get far with education, but nowadays this is far from the truth. Many people get in by who they know, education just doesn't cut it anymore. To be honest many companies have said you need experience to get an internship, which doesn't seem right. Why even call it an internship?

According to the U.S. Bureau of Labor Statistics (BLS), finance majors must possess at least a bachelor's degree (4 year degree) in finance, business administration, accounting, and/or economics. The finance majors with a master's degree (6-7 year degree) have a better chance of getting the positions over the finance majors with a bachelor's degree. If a finance major would like to move up into higher positions a master's degree is required unless one's experience can substitute for the master's degree (rarely). For a better foundation, a finance major may want to consider a designation, such as the Chartered Financial Analyst (CFA) designation. The more education the more opportunities a finance major has in obtaining employment and receiving promotions within their organization.

I think the BLS needs to check and filter in the "who you know" aspect of getting a job. I guarantee, if you ask people how they got their jobs, they will say someone they knew helped them or directed them to the right person. Some probably got their education on the job or through college during the job.

A finance major can find a various amount of titles in the finance functions of a company. The finance positions in a company can range from entry-level positions to management positions, with many years of experience and education the position of Chief Executive Officer (CEO) is attainable. Most finance majors can find job opportunities in banks; mutual funds, and other kinds of financial institutions; or in government or some kind of charitable organization. Titles held in finance departments are as follows:

- **Financial Analyst**

- **Personal Financial Advisor**

- **Financial Manager**

- **Budget Analyst**

- **Cost Estimator**

- **Financial Examiners**

- **Accountant**

- **Insurance Underwriters**

- **Securities, Commodities, and Financial Services Sales Agents**

- **Financial Article Writers**

These are just to name a few titles a finance major can hold in the finance department of many organizations. Each title holds its own specific job description.

Financial Analysts

A Financial Analyst's job description varies by company, but here are a few key responsibilities:

•   Monitor developments in the fields of industrial technology, business, finance, and economic theory.

•   Prepare plans of action for investment, using financial analyses.

•   Monitor fundamental economic, industrial, and corporate developments by analyzing information from financial publications and services, investment banking firms, government agencies, trade publications, company sources, or personal interviews.

•   Determine the prices at which securities should be syndicated and offered to the public.

•   Recommend investments and investment timing to companies, investment firm staff, or the public.

•   Draw charts and graphs, using computer spreadsheets, to illustrate technical reports.

•   Contact brokers and purchase investments for companies, according to company policy.

•   Evaluate and compare the relative quality of various securities in a given industry.

•   Present oral or written reports on general economic trends, individual corporations, and entire industries.

•   Interpret data on price, yield, stability, future investment-risk trends, economic influences, and other factors affecting investment programs.

- Inform investment decisions by analyzing financial information to forecast business, industry, or economic conditions.

- Collaborate with investment bankers to attract new corporate clients to securities firms.

Personal Financial Advisors

A Personal Financial Advisor's job description varies by company, but here are a few of the key responsibilities:

- Devise debt liquidation plans that include payoff priorities and timelines.

- Prepare or interpret for clients' information such as investment performance reports, financial document summaries, or income projections.

- Explain and document for clients the types of services that are to be provided, and the responsibilities to be taken by the personal financial advisor.

- Build and maintain client bases, keeping current client plans up-to-date and recruiting new clients on an ongoing basis.

- Recommend strategies clients can use to achieve their financial goals and objectives, including specific recommendations in such areas as cash management, insurance coverage, and investment planning.

- Research and investigate available investment opportunities to determine whether they fit into financial plans.

- Determine amounts of aid to be granted to students, considering such factors as funds available, extent of demand, and financial needs.

- Interview clients to determine their current income, expenses, insurance coverage, tax status, financial objectives, risk tolerance, or other information needed to develop a financial plan.

- Review clients' accounts and plans regularly to determine whether life changes, economic changes, or financial performance indicate a need for plan reassessment.

- Guide clients in the gathering of information, such as bank account records, income tax returns, life and disability insurance records, pension plans, or wills.

- Contact clients periodically to determine any changes in their financial status.

- Implement financial planning recommendations or refer clients to someone who can assist them with plan implementation.

- Meet with clients' other advisors, such as attorneys, accountants, trust officers, or investment bankers, to fully understand clients' financial goals and circumstances.

- Monitor financial market trends to ensure that plans are effective, and to identify any necessary updates.

- Sell financial products such as stocks, bonds, mutual funds, and insurance if licensed to do so.

- Collect information from students to determine their eligibility for specific financial aid programs.

- Conduct seminars or workshops on financial planning topics, such as retirement planning, estate planning, or the evaluation of severance packages.

- Explain to individuals and groups the details of financial assistance available to college and university students, such as loans, grants, and scholarships.

- Answer clients' questions about the purposes and details of financial plans and strategies.

- Analyze financial information obtained from clients to determine strategies for meeting clients' financial objectives.

- Open accounts for clients and disburse funds from accounts to creditors as agent for clients.

Financial Managers

A Financial Manager's job responsibilities are the same across the board, but just a little difference depending on company:

- Plan, direct, and coordinate risk and insurance programs of establishments to control risks and losses.

- Establish procedures for custody and control of assets, records, loan collateral, and securities, in order to ensure safekeeping.

- Evaluate data pertaining to costs in order to plan budgets.

- Evaluate financial reporting systems, accounting and collection procedures, and investment activities, and make recommendations for changes to procedures, operating systems, budgets, and other financial control functions.

- Review reports of securities transactions and price lists in order to analyze market conditions.

- Direct floor operations of brokerage firm engaged in buying and selling securities at exchange.

- Network within communities to find and attract new business.

- Approve or reject, or coordinate the approval and rejection of, lines of credit and commercial, real estate, and personal loans.

- Plan, direct, and coordinate the activities of workers in branches, offices, or departments of such establishments as branch banks, brokerage firms, risk and insurance departments, or credit departments.

- Oversee the flow of cash and financial instruments.

- Develop and analyze information to assess the current and future financial status of firms.

- Monitor order flow and transactions that brokerage firm executes on the floor of exchange.

- Submit delinquent accounts to attorneys or outside agencies for collection.

- Prepare financial and regulatory reports required by laws, regulations, and boards of directors.

- Prepare operational and risk reports for management analysis.

- Communicate with stockholders and other investors to provide information, and to raise capital.

- Analyze and classify risks and investments to determine their potential impacts on companies.

- Direct insurance negotiations, select insurance brokers and carriers, and place insurance.

- Establish and maintain relationships with individual and business customers, and provide assistance with problems these customers may encounter.

- Examine, evaluate, and process loan applications.

- Recruit staff members, and oversee training programs.

- Review collection reports to determine the status of collections and the amounts of outstanding balances.

Budget Analysts

A Budget Analyst's job description varies by company a well, but here are a few key responsibilities:

- Examine budget estimates for completeness, accuracy, and conformance with procedures and regulations.

- Seek new ways to improve efficiency and increase profits.

- Consult with managers to ensure that budget adjustments are made in accordance with program changes.

- Match appropriations for specific programs with appropriations for broader programs, including items for emergency funds.

- Interpret budget directives and establish policies for carrying out directives.

- Direct the preparation of regular and special budget reports.

- Analyze monthly department budgeting and accounting reports to maintain expenditure controls.

- Compile and analyze accounting records and other data to determine the financial resources required to implement a program.

- Summarize budgets and submit recommendations for the approval or disapproval of funds requests.

- Testify before examining and fund-granting authorities, clarifying and promoting the proposed budgets.

- Review operating budgets to analyze trends affecting budget needs.

- Provide advice and technical assistance with cost analysis, fiscal allocation, and budget preparation.

- Perform cost-benefit analyses to compare operating programs, review financial requests, or explore alternative financing methods.

Cost Estimators

A Cost Estimator's job description varies by company and industry, but the basics are the same:

- Prepare cost and expenditure statements and other necessary documentation at regular intervals for the duration of the project.

- Establish and maintain tendering process, and conduct negotiations.

- Prepare estimates used by management for purposes such as planning, organizing, and scheduling work.

- Prepare estimates for use in selecting vendors or subcontractors.

- Review material and labor requirements, to decide whether it is more cost-effective to produce or purchase components.

- Consult with clients, vendors, personnel in other departments or construction foremen to discuss and formulate estimates and resolve issues.

- Visit site and record information about access, drainage and topography, and availability of services such as water and electricity.

- Prepare and maintain a directory of suppliers, contractors and subcontractors.

- Set up cost monitoring and reporting systems and procedures.

- Analyze blueprints and other documentation to prepare time, cost, materials, and labor estimates.

- Confer with engineers, architects, owners, contractors and subcontractors on changes and adjustments to cost estimates.

- Conduct special studies to develop and establish standard hour and related cost data or to effect cost reduction.

- Assess cost effectiveness of products, projects or services, tracking actual costs relative to bids as the project develops.

Financial Examiners

A Financial Examiners job responsibilities consists of:

• Evaluate internal and external audit reports, balance sheets, expense accounts, operating income accounts, tax documents, and special reports reflecting assets and liabilities.

• Confirm the authenticity and accuracy of financial records, and ensure that the organization they are investigating is financially solvent.

• Conduct interviews with financial managers responsible for overseeing financial transactions.

• Go over the minutes of meetings of directors, stockholders and committees in order to investigate the specific authority extended at various levels of management.

• Scrutinize financial reports and records to ensure compliance.

• Request transactions reports to ensure they are being processed correctly.

• Review accounts on an individual basis to ensure compliance.

• Establish guidelines for procedures and policies that comply with new and revised regulations, and direct their implementation.

• Review and analyze new, proposed, or revised laws, regulations, policies, and procedures.

• Participate in meetings with bank directors and trustees.

• Analyze applications dealing with mergers, acquisitions, establishment of new institutions, and acceptance in Federal Reserve System or registration of securities sales in order to determine their public interest value and conformance to regulations, and recommend acceptance or rejection.

•   Check filings for accuracy and make changes when necessary, and provide recommendations for ensuring compliance with laws and regulations.

•   Analyze audit reports and recommend improvements to internal processes.

Accountants

An Accountant's job description varies by title, which makes the responsibilities differ. An overall Accountant's responsibilities are:

•   Audits contracts, orders, and vouchers, and prepares reports to substantiate individual transactions prior to settlement.

•   Analyzes financial information detailing assets, liabilities, and capital, and prepares balance sheet, profit and loss statement, and other reports to summarize current and projected company financial position, using calculator or computer.

•   May establish, modify, document, and coordinate implementation of accounting and accounting control procedures.

•   May direct and coordinate activities of other accountants and clerical workers performing accounting and bookkeeping tasks.

•   Applies principles of accounting to analyze financial information and prepare financial reports: Compiles and analyzes financial information to prepare entries to accounts, such as general ledger accounts, documenting business transactions.

- May devise and implement manual or computer-based system for general accounting.

Underwriter

An Underwriter's job description varies by company, but the responsibilities are similar if not the same:

- Selecting appropriate and competitive premiums based on information and judgment.

- Deciding whether the risk should be shared with a re-insurer.

- Studying insurance proposals.

- Deciding how much should be paid out.

- Negotiating terms.

- Calculating the risk.

- Liaising with professionals and specialists to help judge risk assessment.

- Writing policies and adding specific conditions when required.

- Assessing background information on the client.

Financial Services Sales Agent

A Financial Services Sales Agent's job description varies by what their title, company, and product:

- Build relationships with clients and communities.

- Determine clients' financial needs and areas of improvement.

- Provide solutions for short and long-term financial goals.

- Present products and services via a presentation or slideshow.

- Determine security risks.

- Use financial, tax, economics and accounting skills to review a client's personal data and recommend investment strategies that are appropriate to the client's goals.

- Recommend certain services such as life insurance, retirement income, investments, and long-term care insurance.

- Negotiate sales agreements and contracts.

- Take payments.

- Sell financial services to businesses and individuals.

- Develop prospects from current commercial customers, referral leads, and sales and trade meetings.

- Prepare forms or agreements.

- Sell trusts, investments, and check processing services.

- Determine future growth.

- Help clients achieve financial security.

- Advise customers regarding expected fluctuations.

- Evaluate financial reporting systems, accounting and collection procedures, and investment activities, and make recommendations for changes to procedures, operating systems, budgets, and other financial control functions.

- Solicit business, authorize loans, and direct the investment of funds, always adhering to Federal and State laws and regulations.

- Advise a client on whether to buy certain types of stocks, bonds and mutual funds.

- Make presentations on financial services to groups in order to attract new clients.

- Determine whether loans must be obtained to meet cash requirements or whether surplus cash can be invested.

Financial Article Writer

Financial Article Writers can write many kinds of articles like freelance articles for websites. Some of the responsibilities include:

- Writing financial documents, news items, articles or study material.

- Keeping updated on various financial regulatory and global activities.

- Keeping watch on various global stock markets

- Working on special financial projects.

- Writing various financial documents for clients like banks, agencies, or insurance agencies.

- Developing content for print, online, and presentation materials.

- Writing copy for website postings and articles.

- Coordinating with various department members and senior financial writers.

Here are a few articles I wrote for The Motley Fool a while ago:

1.   The Elephant in the Room

2.   Should You Get Out of BlackBerry?

3.   Amazon Should Get in this Tornado

4.   Why This Company Said, "Faster is Better!"

The Elephant in the Room

Lately, IT services have been the talk across the board. With emerging markets popping up everywhere you look, IT services companies are trying to expand and set a mark in the markets. The International Data Corporation (IDC) estimated that in 2011, the total market was more than $855 billion, and estimates that can flourish at a compound annual growth rate of 4.6% through 2018. Cognizant (NASDAQ: CTSH) is one of those IT services companies that is already on the rise along with IDC's estimates.

In the know

Cognizant provides consulting, business process outsourcing services, and information technology, with the intent to aid the world's leading companies in building a more robust business. Cognizant blends a passion for deep industry and business process expertise, technology innovation, client satisfaction, and a global, collaborative workforce that includes the future of work. Cognizant has over 50 delivery centers worldwide, with its headquarters in Teaneck, New Jersey.

Cognizant has a market cap of $22 billion and a trailing twelve month P/E ratio of 20, against an industry average of 18.80. Q1 2013 EPS was $0.93, compared to that of Q1 2012 coming in at $0.79, a 15% increase. Analysts think earnings will continue to grow over the next several years giving Cognizant a five-year PEG ratio just under 1.

Buy and hold investors should be excited about a company with a good looking estimates future.

Savvy numbers

"Our performance during the first-quarter of 2013 was strong, and we are encouraged by the healthy demand for our broad range of services," Chief Executive Francisco D'Souza said in the 8-K quarterly report filed on May 8, 2013.

Cognizant's revenue rose to $2.02 billion in Q1 2013 up 3.7% successively and 18.1% year-over-year. Cognizant had $1.5 million in cash on hand and working capital (Total Current Assets – Total Current Liabilities) of $3.6 million in Q1 2013. Cognizant had no short-term debt or long-term debt for Q1 2013, or for fiscal 2009 through fiscal 2012. Cognizant intends on utilizing its cash on hand for expansion of current operations, embodying its offshore development and delivery centers, enduring development of new service lines, potential acquisitions of related businesses, development of joint ventures, stock repurchases and general corporate purposes, including working capital.

Wipro (NYSE: WIT) just one of many of Cognizant's rivals is facing a terrible time in its business. In Q1 2013 Wipro's revenue had declined by 6% to $7 billion from $7.3 billion in Q1 2012, depending on government and telecom spending, which was weak. Furthermore, Wipro's management set guidance for revenue growth between -0.6% and 1.6% for this fiscal year, which is kind of discouraging once compared to that of the expected industry average of 12%-14% set by the National Association of Software and Services Companies (NASSCOM).

Cognizant have been continuing penetration of the European and the rest of the world (primarily the Asia Pacific) markets where it also experienced revenue growth of 22.7% and 35.4%, respectively. It has seen sustained strength in the North America market where its revenues grew 16.3%, or $221.5 million and increased customer spending on discretionary projects.

Cognizant has augmented penetration at its existing customers, including strategic clients. Cognizant finished the quarter with roughly 1,000 active clients, compared to roughly 805 in Q1 2012, and increased the number of strategic clients by seven during the quarter, bringing the total amount of its strategic clients to 221. Cognizant describes a strategic client as one offering the potential to generate a minimum of $5 million to $50 million or more in annual revenues at maturity.

Kid in a candy store

When kids go into a candy store they run all over the place, overwhelmed by all the candy in their peripheral vision. Like kids in a candy store, Cognizant is scouring every area it can to expand its business.

Cognizant's current India real estate development program embodies planned construction of 10.5 million square feet of new space between 2011 and the end of 2015. The program embodies the expected expenditure of over $700 million during this period on land acquisition, facilities construction, and furnishings to build new company-owned state-of-the-art development and delivery centers in regions primarily designated as Special Economic Zones, located in India.

On February 28, 2013, Cognizant finished the acquisition of six additional companies. The transaction strengthened its local presence in Switzerland and Germany and expanded its expertise in enterprise application services and high-end testing services. Cognizant has also invested in developing the Future of Work called SMAC (Social, Mobile, Analytics and Cloud), which is one combined stack, where each function permits another to amplify its effect.

Cognizant has expanded its service offerings, including Consulting, Information Technology Infrastructure Services, and Business Process Outsourcing services, which enabled it to cross-sell new services to its customers and meet the rapidly growing demand for complex large-scale outsourcing solutions.

The Board of Directors increased the stock repurchase program by $500 million, from $1 billion to $1.5 billion, and extended the term of the program to December 31, 2014. As of May 8, 2013, it has repurchased $940 million of its shares under its repurchase program.

The Foolish bottom line

Cognizant is one of many IT services companies expected to grow for years to come. Analysts give CTSH a price target of $79 for 2013, but I think it will surpass this amount. Cognizant has grown year-over-year without default and most likely will continue to grow on a constant basis.

This IT services company is stepping its game up trying to set in stone its mark in the emerging markets, like India and elsewhere. As long as the IT services industry expands its growth, so will a

company like Cognizant, adapting to all new changes
with immense modifications.

☐

Should You Get Out of BlackBerry?

Many companies go public to decrease debt or to obtain financing externally, instead of using the banking system. A company has many other reasons to want to go public instead of staying private, like public credibility, the ability to offer stock and stock options to attract top talent, and the ability to offer securities instead of 100% capital for acquisitions of other companies. BlackBerry (NASDAQ: BBRY) is thinking of going private because it cannot keep up with competitors like Apple (NASDAQ: AAPL) and Samsung (NASDAQOTH: SSNLF), among other issues.

Private companies have 100% authority over its operational choices and it does not have to worry about shareholder interference and expectations. As an owner of a privately held company, you cannot have your company sold out from under you. Disclosures about a private company's operations are not called for with private companies, these are just a few private company benefits. BlackBerry has many issues, but could going private help it solve its problems?

Breathing room

A little breathing room might not be enough, but the CEO and the Board of Directors are in private conversation on going private. This breathing room can give BlackBerry a chance to survive and fix issues it has.

January 2012, BlackBerry spoke with Silver Lake a private-equity firm, about the possibility of going private. The conversation fell through because the companies could not agree on the valuation of BlackBerry. A period of breathing room could give the company more time to have talks with Silver Lake and other companies. Enterprise computing has been the primary discussion between Silver Lake and BlackBerry as of lately.

Enterprise computing is a computing model where many users have a passage to data and applications saved on a single server.

This period of breathing room can give BlackBerry enough time to sale some of its patents or expand its BlackBerry 10 OS. The company could finally find a way to structure a deal, which at this point has been a dead end. BlackBerry has high-margin services business and a high value patent portfolio that could draw attention from other tech companies. This breathing room will allow BlackBerry to proceed as usual, without explaining or telling shareholders how the company is running its operations or what deals are on the table.

Losing on all fronts

BlackBerry's new smartphone has not lived up to what BlackBerry thought or hoped it would. Sales have failed to meet expectations and the stock has dropped dramatically by more than 20% this year alone. Its market cap has fallen to $4.95 billion from its high in 2008 of around $84 billion, while Apple has seen 0.9% growth in its OEM market share, looking at comScore's stats chart.

Top Smartphone OEMs 3 Month Avg. Ending Jun. 2013 vs. 3 Month Avg. Ending Mar. 2013 Total U.S. Smartphone Subscribers Age 13+ Source: comScore MobiLens			
	Share (%) of Smartphone Subscribers		
	Mar-13	Jun-13	Point Change
Total Mobile Subscribers	100.0%	100.0%	N/A
Apple	39.0%	39.9%	0.9
Samsung	21.7%	23.7%	2.0
HTC	9.0%	8.5%	-0.5
Motorola	8.5%	7.2%	-1.3
LG	6.8%	6.6%	-0.2

Source: comSCORE, Aug. 9, 2013

LG, Motorola, and HTC have lost market share, thus helping Apple and Samsung gain more market share. As you can see, Samsung is up 2% taking majority of the lost market share.

Apple may be in the lead when it comes to all OEMs, but when it comes to operating systems, Apple is in second when compared to Google's Android, but grasping majority of the lost market share from

BlackBerry and Symbian.

Top Smartphone Platforms 3 Month Avg. Ending Jun. 2013 vs. 3 Month Avg. Ending Mar. 2013 Total U.S. Smartphone Subscribers Age 13+ Source: comScore MobiLens	Share (%) of Smartphone Subscribers		
	Mar-13	Jun-13	Point Change
Total Smartphone Subscribers	100.0%	100.0%	N/A
Android	52.0%	52.0%	0.0
Apple	39.0%	39.9%	0.9
BlackBerry	5.2%	4.4%	-0.8
Microsoft	3.0%	3.1%	0.1
Symbian	0.5%	0.3%	-0.2

Source: comSCORE, Aug. 9, 2013

The Z10 smartphone's price was reduced to $49.99 amid comatose sales. Upon its debut in March in the U.S., the smartphone went on sale for $199. I hope it costs less to build the device than what the device is selling for now. Apple sells one million tablets in at least a week and Blackberry's Playbook has finally reached over one million customers, which is terrible.

Units of the Galaxy S4 have not sold, as the company would have liked, but the company still has more market share than BlackBerry. Samsung has been going under an inventory correction because its devices are not moving as fast as usual. Samsung usually tries to flood consumers with multiple devices, while Apple only puts out one or two devices a year in every segment it has.

The foolish bottom line

BlackBerry may need to consider licensing its software to other tech giants like Samsung or whoever. Apple and Samsung can grab whatever sales the BB10 devices have, if nothing comes out of Blackberry going private. With its sales, market cap, and revenue dwindling away, coming up with ways to generate new revenue should be an option.

Aug. 8, 2013, BlackBerry reported that the U.S. Defense Information System Agency gave it thumbs up on its first two BB10 mobile devices to be used on Department of Defense networks, affirming that the BB10 devices has all required security measures set in place. This is a win-win for BlackBerry, although it seems late in the game, but it is never too late to try.

Apple and Samsung would be at least 25% of the reason for the fall of BlackBerry, if it were to fail. BlackBerry and its lack of focus on what consumers want is a major flaw in its problems. I watched a movie called "Margin Call" and the CEO said, "It sure is a lot easier to be first." BlackBerry was last in every aspect of smartphone innovation and tablets; maybe the breathing period is necessary for restructuring the way the company looks at things. BlackBerry has not yet decided if its going private or not, but it is something to watch going forward.

□

Amazon Should Get in This Tornado

As we all know, BlackBerry (NASDAQ: BBRY) is in a crisis and in need of some help. Conversations on going private, acquisition, and more of the like, does this company have a clue as to what it should do? At one point or another, it was a stock market honeybunch, but now it has been oozing out market share to the likes of smartphones utilizing Google's Android operating system and Apple (NASDAQ: AAPL). To top that off, its new BB10 smartphones have not gained any suction with smartphone consumers.

Private conversation tornado

Just last week, there was news that BlackBerry was holding private conversations about going private. If BlackBerry were to go private, it would have 100% authority over all its operational decisions and it would not have to be vexed about shareholder hindrance and expectancies. If you owned a private company, you would not have to be worried about your company being sold right from underneath you. BlackBerry would not have to disclose anything about its business to the SEC or the public.

This is not the first time BlackBerry has thought of going private, in January of 2012, BlackBerry held conversations with Silver Lake, which is a private-equity firm, about possibly going private. The discussion subsided because neither company could come to an agreement on BlackBerry's valuation.

BlackBerry could go private and fix its issues, regroup, and find a buyer or private-equity firm. It could magnify its BB10 operating system or sale a few of its patents. BlackBerry could seek out deals because it has high-margin services business units and a high value patent portfolio, which could generate assiduity from other private-equity tech firms or tech companies.

Acquisition conversation tornado

Who would or could buy BlackBerry? Microsoft, Lenovo, other Chinese manufacturers, or Amazon (NASDAQ: AMZN) could buy the company, and since Amazon is in the market for a passage into the smartphone arena, it would be the best candidate. In 2012, Amazon attempted to acquire BlackBerry, but it declined takeover propositions from Amazon and other plausible acquirers. The Canadian government will vet any foreign takeover of a Canadian firm. In the past, the Canadian government has characterized BlackBerry as a Canadian royalty.

Amazon's mobile redeeming feature is the Kindle, what the iPod did for Apple is what the Kindle did for Amazon. The only difference was that Amazon, by this time was on the upturn, while Apple required a propeller at the time. The main reason the introduction of the Kindle was so powerful was that Amazon, by that time was the world's dominant online retailer – for products, and not just eBooks or physical books.

Apple is unmatched when it comes to app sales, digital music sales, and is possibly gaining ground on eBooks. Apple is a service, while Amazon is a marketplace. Apple can only sale you technology, and digital content such as, information and media. On the other hand Amazon can sale you physical products, Google Products, and Apple products. If you wanted food, you could purchase that too along with many other things on Amazon's marketplace.

Amazon plus BlackBerry combined

If Amazon acquired BlackBerry there would be many things offered to consumers. BlackBerry's data security, accompanying patents, and software warrant another blanket of protection to Amazon customers utilizing its services on any tech device. BlackBerry has a collection of patents and Amazon is already a trusted marketplace. This combination strengthens the unbroken levels of trust Amazon customers will have when maintaining financial transactions, transferring, records, and processing.

BlackBerry has procured technologies affiliated with transfiguring and emending documents on handheld devices and transforming to accustomed layouts. Amazon's cloud is an excellent repository and excellent for reviewing files, but not able to make revisions while on the go. BlackBerry's patents will permit Amazon to produce a more vigorous cloud platform without third-party apps on tablets and mobile devices.

The Kindle Fire relies heavily on Android because Amazon does not own a mobile software solution. If it were to make its own hardware and provide its own service, it would need the end-user encounter manufactured from the bottom up to coordinate, a la Apple. This will thus render Amazon the acuteness to fulfill expeditiously and contend with both Google and Apple in the handheld device arena with consolidated services like Amazon's cloud. Amazon could replace the BlackBerry business solutions and software to tally in services like Kindle libraries and Amazon Prime Video with a system that is guarded and sheltered.

What Apple and Google cannot provide Amazon can, a marketplace! Amazon could come to be a determinant for access controls, users, history, organize purchases, and procurement. People who make purchases from travel expenses to office supplies on a budget, can be organized securely and tracked digitally. Finally yet importantly, BlackBerry's contracts with government departments and companies will complement Amazon's current bag of software solutions it renders to the Department of Agriculture, Energy, Treasury, and State.

The Foolish bottom line

BlackBerry is already going down and Amazon is currently the point of sale for more types of products than any other marketplace on the planet. Amazon could take the smartphone industry far into the future and an acquisition of BlackBerry guarantees a level of efficiency and security that Amazon needs for speedy advancement and employment.

Moreover, if Amazon entered into the smartphone arena, vicissitude among Amazon, Google, Apple, and other OEM's will catapult us into a place that for now we can only day dream of. Mobile consumer products, services, and technology are investments for the future, the acquisition or merger of BlackBerry and Amazon will help investors make beaucoup loads of money.

Why this Company Said, "Faster is Better!"

There have always been discussions over slow internet speeds and "faster is better" is overwhelmingly the winner. Recently, Google (NASDAQ: GOOG) struck a deal with Starbucks (NASDAQ: SBUX) to provide free high-speed Wi-Fi service in all 7,000 U.S. Starbucks. Google and Level 3 Communications (NYSE: LVLT) will start this project this month at Starbucks' busiest shops, meaning the shops with the highest Wi-Fi usage, not the shops with the most revenue coming in.

Slow but useful

Any person that does not have internet when on the road or at home will most likely go to a place like Starbucks for free internet service provided by AT&T (NYSE: T). It does not matter if the service is slow or not because it's free, but yes, the slower the network speeds the less you can do. Of course it's good for engaging in some minor Web surfing, or checking your email, but attempting to take part in a video conference, or Skype call would prove to be senseless. The freezing, blurred buffering video, and rippled audio is extremely frustrating on both ends of the camera.

If you were trying to download a file or something that was 7 GB on a slow network, it would take a while. Even small downloads on slow networks take a while, but "something is better than nothing," is what most people would probably say. AT&T helped Starbucks become an ideal "office space" for those without an office or internet service.

Faster is always better

Google and Level 3 are offering a newer network that will be about 10 times faster, thus making Starbucks an increasingly more attractive "office space" for migrant business customers. With a 10 times faster network, Starbucks won't just be accommodating anymore, it will be the predominant haven for mobile and remote users.

With the faster network speeds you can download colossal presentations faster than you can drink a glass of Iced White Chocolate Mocha. This quicker internet speed will make it viable to link to virtualized applications, or virtual servers and work continuously like your seated right next to the server.

Many Starbucks customers in Austin, Kansas City, and Provo, Utah are serviced by Google's Google Fiber. Starbucks' shift from AT&T to Google will give these areas increased speed of around100 times. I think I might move into one of these locations if my internet speed will be that fast.

Out with the old, in with the new

AT&T speeds were slow with a T1 line for 1.5 megabit speeds, while Google and Level 3 are offering speeds of about 10 times as fast and 100 times as fast in certain locations. AT&T did not go without a fight, AT&T did offer to upgrade its Wi-Fi speeds up to 10 times as fast, but 100 times as fast is far more intriguing and AT&T could not offer that. AT&T will continue to accommodate Starbucks with an assortment of other services over its improved network, including its supposed most fast and reliable 4G LTE network.

Google will bring in its faster internet speeds, which could possibly bring more customers to Starbucks. Google also partnered with Starbucks to develop

Starbucks Digital Network to help offer free and fascinating Internet content for all Starbucks' shops. Level 3 is going to upgrade all 7,000 Starbucks' shops with high bandwidth connectivity and new routing equipment, plus manage in-store connectivity.

Google has been in the business of trying to help the Internet grow more tenaciously by investing in projects to make the Internet more widely available, cheaper, and have speedier access. Just recently Google gave $600,000 to San Francisco to bring free Wi-Fi to 31 public parks.

The Foolish Bottom Line

As mobile phone carriers shy away from providing unlimited data plans for smartphone devices, Starbucks can attract those customers with faster internet speeds. Starbucks' revenues will soon rise because of this type of improvement in its stores, thus sending its stock through the roof, a ride I'm willing to take.

Google is always a buy in its efforts to take over the world or have its paw print on everything moving. From investing in internet services, providing smartphones, advertisement, or internet search, it has always been on investor's minds.

This project may give Level 3 the boost it needs as it claims to be the largest backbone for the internet. The company may be in the red for now, but this project may turn the red into green. AT&T still has its foot print in Starbucks, so don't let the news of it losing its Wi-Fi partnership get you down.

These positions are held by finance majors working for security and commodity brokerages, banks and credit institutions, insurance carriers, private industries, and for government. Majority of these positions can be found in major financial centers (e.g. New York City). All businesses employ finance majors except for some businesses that prefer to do the financial functions on their own. These positions require business attire for work. The work hours for these positions are usually 40 hours a week but depending on the choice of title, hours can exceed the normal 40 hours. The 40 hours is the base, but hours can reach 50 or more hours per week. The work environment is usually in office but some positions require travel during the work week.

Salaries for finance majors in the financial industry differ substantially on the basis of career selection. Nonetheless, finance majors can anticipate on earning $50,000 plus per annum. The mean per annum salaries for these finance titles as of May 2010 according to the U.S. Bureau of Labor Statistics (www.bls.gov) are as follows:

- Financial Analyst: $74,350

- Personal Financial Advisor: $64,750

- Financial Manager: $103,910

- Budget Analyst: $68,200

- Cost Estimators: $57, 860

- Financial Examiners: $74,940

- Accountant: $61,690

- Insurance Underwriters: $59,290

- Securities, Commodities, and Financial Services Sales Agents: $70,190

- Financial Article Writers: Up to you and how much you decide to write

Don't forget to add in the bonuses some of these positions offer.